Allah SubhanaHu Ta'ala

SALAH

HOW GOD TEACHES US TO PRAY, HOW TO PRAY WITH THE HOLY QURAN

ILLUSTRATED BY OKAY ALTINISIK

This Booklet is also available as ebook.

Translated & Illustrated by Dr Okay Altinisik

Printed on recycled paper

ISBN: 978-3-9504862-8-5

The Golden Light

Follow these step-by-step illustrations to learn and to teach your children the correct way of ablution and worship, which **G**od revealed nowhere other than in the Holy Quran. By using nothing except **A**llah's pure and unchanged Verses, this Booklet purifies our most sacred Deed from the falsehoods which have been accumulating over a thousand years, such as calling someone else alongside **G**od in the adhan, which is forbidden in Sura Al Jinn, The Genies, 72:18, or addressing someone else in the shahadah, which is practiced by sunnites, shiites and sufis, and similarly by Christians, which is technically no different from polytheism and which is the only thing "**A**llah forgives not" according to Sura An-Nisa, The Women, 4:48. Someone who "submits" to **G**od, a "Muslim", does not pray by manmade instructions, she or he prays exclusively with our **L**ord's true Instructions, Glory to Him, the Exalted **O**ne. While sunnites, shiites and sufis deny that these exist and use the fake sayings of

Prophet Muhammad to learn worshiping, this Booklet either proves that they contradict **A**llah's Book or that they do not read it at all.

Since no one except **G**od authored the Great "Quran", which is Arabic for "Recitation", beware that reciting Him is a strict Ritual,
thus no one other than "the cleansed ones" are allowed to touch it, be it an eBook or a paperback Version –Sura Al Waqiah, The Occurrence, 56:79. This simply means that you will need to wash your face, arms and feet if you want to open the Holy Book to memorize a Verse in order to pray the Way **G**od wants you to pray.

Sincerely, Dr Okay Altinisik

Audhu Billahi
mina ashshaytani
arrajeemi

In **A**llah I seek
refuge from satan,
the cursed one

Biismi A**llahi**
ArRahmani
ArRaheemi

In the Name of
Allah, the
Merciful, the
Compassionate **O**ne

So glorify your **L**ord with Praise and be from the ones prostrating themselves, and worship your **L**ord until Certainty come to you.

Sura Al Hijr | The Hindrance 15:98-99

And your **L**ord decided that you worship not except, oh yes, Him...

Sura Al Isra | The Night Journey 17:23

And before **A**llah prostrates himself whoever be in the Heavens and on, earth, willingly and reluctantly, and their shadows, on the morning errand and in the late afternoons.

Sura Ar-Rad | The Thunder 13:15

So Glory to **A**llah the time you enter into evening and the time you enter upon morning; and for Him is the Praise in the Heavens and on earth and in the evening and the time you enter midday.

Sura Ar-Rum | The Romans 30:17-18

Oh whichever be here of

those who–who believed,

when you rose to prayer...

... then wash your faces...

... and your
hands until
the elbows,
and rub
your heads...

and your feet until both ankles. And the polluted one, so clean yourselves if you were. And if you were ill or on a journey, or someone from you came from the sinking, or you touched the women, then you find not any water, then you aim at pure soil. So rub your faces and your hands among it. **A**llah wants not to bring about of any anguish upon you, and yet, He wants to purify you and to complete His Blessing upon you, perhaps you are grateful.

Sura Al Maidah | The Table 5:6

And your **L**ord, so magnify, and your clothing, so purge, and uncleanness, so desert...

Sura Al Muddathir | The One Who is Enveloping Himself 74:3-5

... verily, I–I am your **L**ord, so slip off both of your sandals... And, "I–I chose you... Truly, I–I am **A**llah —no **G**od is except I— so worship me and establish prayer for my Remembrance.

Sura Ta Ha 20:12-14

... we see your face in turnaround in heaven, so we most surely turn you to a direction with which you be pleased. So turn your face towards the Sacred of the Mosque, and wherever you were, so turn your faces towards it. And truly, those who–who were brought the Book, they surely know that it is the Truth from their **L**ord...

Sura Al Baqarah | The Cow 2:144

Say, "Call **A**llah or call the **M**erciful, Whichever you call, then for Him is the most beautiful of names." And you speak not loud in your prayer, nor speak in a low voice in it, and seek a way between that.

Sura Al Isra | The Night Journey 17:110

So when you read the Quran, then seek Protection in **A**llah from the damned of the satan.

Sura An-Nahl | The Bee 16:98

"ALLAHU AKBAR"
Allah is the Greatest
"Audhu Billahi
In Allah I seek
mina ashshaytani
refuge from satan,
arrajeemi"
the cursed one

... and surely, we already brought you seven of the repeated ones and the tremendous of the recitation.

Sura Al Hijr | The Hindrance 15:87

... So recite whatever was possible from the Quran. He knew that there will be the ill among you and other ones who set forth in the land seeking from the Grace of **A**llah, and other ones who fight in the Way of **A**llah. So recite whatever was possible from it and establish prayer and give alms and lend **A**llah a good loan. And whatever you send ahead to yourselves of Goodness, you find it with **A**llah. It is better and greater as pay. And beg Forgiveness from **A**llah —truly, **A**llah is forgiving, compassionate.

Sura Al Muzzammil | The Man Wrapped in His Garments 73:20

"Biismi Allahi ArRahmani ArRaheemi –
In the Name of **A**llah –the **M**erciful, the compassionate **O**ne–,
alhamdu Lillahi Rabbi alaalameena –
Praise to **A**llah –**L**ord of the Worlds,
ArRahmani ArRaheemi – Maleeki yawmi
the **M**erciful, the compassionate **O**ne. **K**ing of the Day
addeeni – iyyaKa naabudu wa iyyaKa
of Judgement, oh yes, You we worship, and, oh yes, You
nastaeenu – ihdina assirata almustaqeema
we beg for help. Guide us on the straight of the path,
– sirata allatheena anaamta aleyhim ghayri
Path of those who-whom You bestowed Favors on, other than
almaghdoobi alayhim wala addalleen"
the disapproved one of them and not of the erring ones.

Sura Al Fatihah | The Opening

1:1-7

“Allahu Akbar –
Allah is the Greatst –
alhamdu Lillahi
Praise to Allah,
Rabbi alaalameena”
Lord of the Worlds

Oh whichever be here of
those who–who believed,
bow down and prostrate
yourselves and worship
your **L**ord and do
Goodness, perhaps you
prosper.

Sura Al Hajj | The Hajj 22:77

"A**llahu Akbar**"

Allah is the Greatest

"Allahu Akbar"

Allah is the Greatest

... Believe in it or you believe not, truly, those who–who were given the Knowledge before it, when it is read to them, they fall down prostrating themselves for the chins and say, "Glory to our **L**ord, verily, the Promise of our **L**ord was surely acted on."

Sura Al Isra | The Night Journey
17:107-108

"Allahu Akbar –
Allah is the Greatest –
subhana Rabbina in
Glory to our **L**ord,
kana waadu
verily, the Promise of
Rabbina
our **L**ord was surely
lamafoolan"
acted on

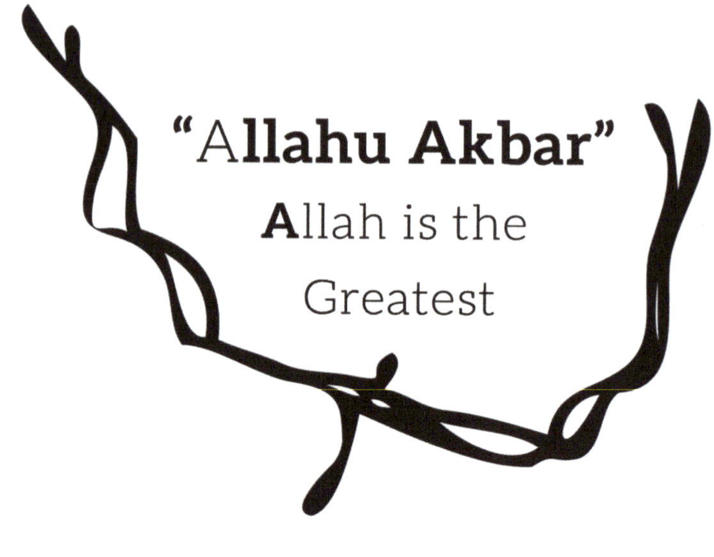
"A**llahu Akbar**"
Allah is the
Greatest

"Allahu Akbar"
Allah is the
Greatest

And they fall down for the chins as they weep, and it increases them in humility.

Sura Al Isra | The Night Journey 17:109

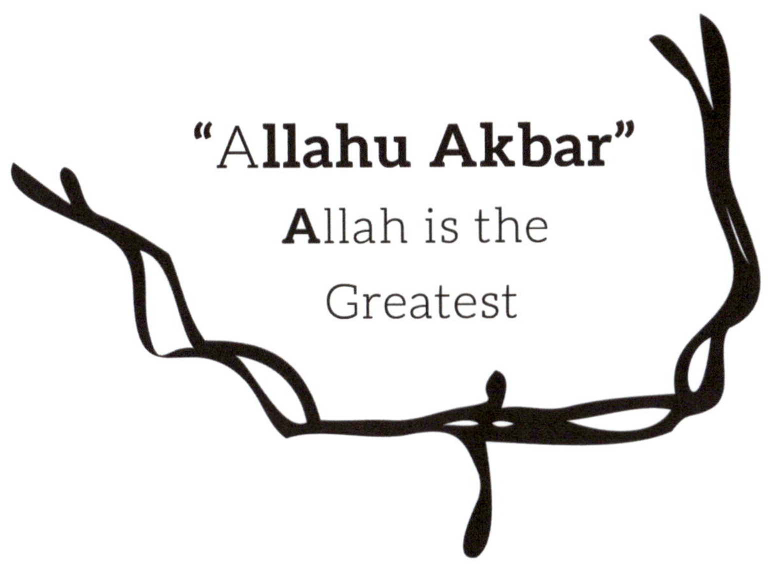

"Allahu Akbar"

Allah is the Greatest

"Biismi Allahi ArRahmani ArRaheemi –

In the Name of **A**llah –the **M**erciful, the compassionate **O**ne–,

qul Huwa Allahu Ahadun –

say, "He is one **A**llah,

Allahu AsSamadu –

Allah the everlasting **O**ne,

lam walid wa lam yulad –

Who beget not, nor be He begotten,

walam yakun laHu kufuan ahadun"

nor be anyone a match for Him."

Sura Al Ikhlas | The Loyalty 112:1-4

“Allahu Akbar –
Allah is the Greatst –
alhamdu Lillahi
Praise to Allah,
Rabbi alaalameena”
Lord of the Worlds

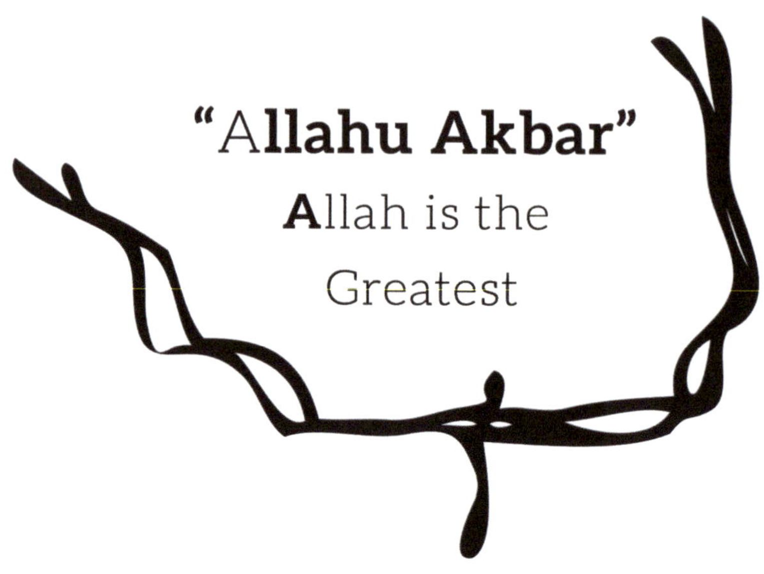

“Allahu Akbar”

Allah is the Greatest

"Allahu Akbar –
Allah is the Greatest –
subhana Rabbina in
Glory to our Lord,
kana waadu
verily, the Promise of
Rabbina
our Lord was surely
lamafoolan"
acted on

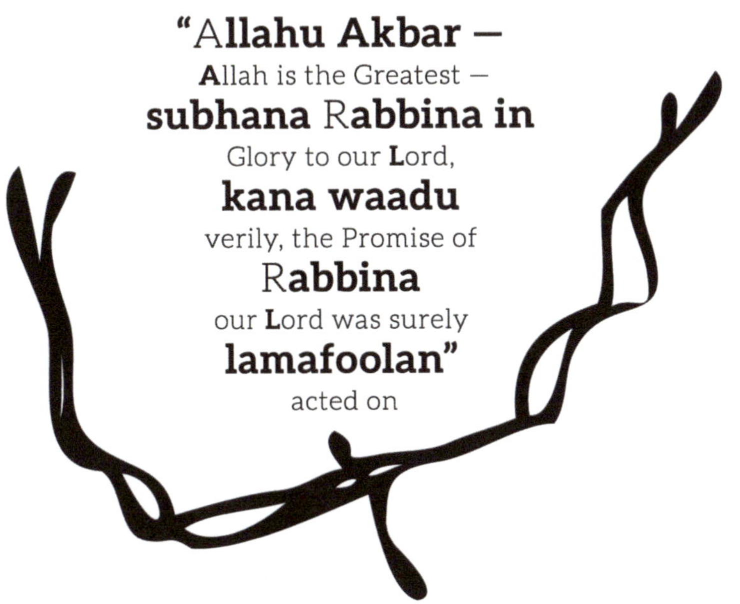

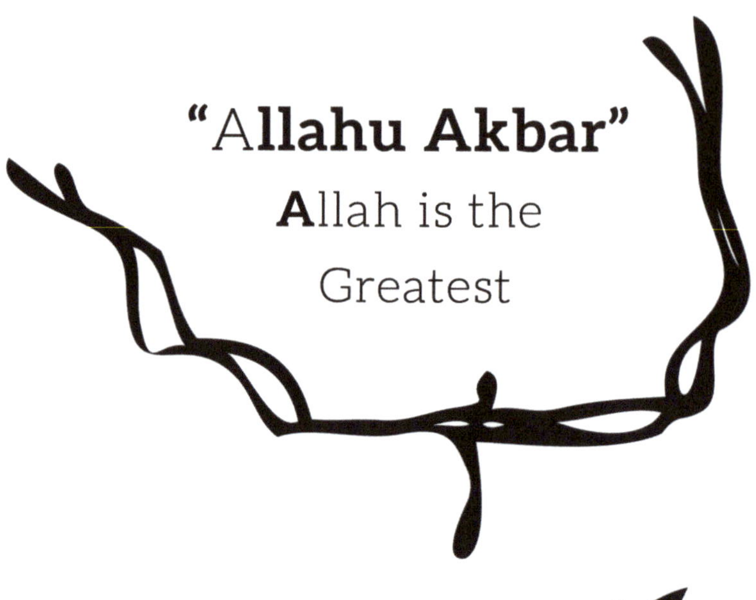
"Allahu Akbar"
Allah is the
Greatest

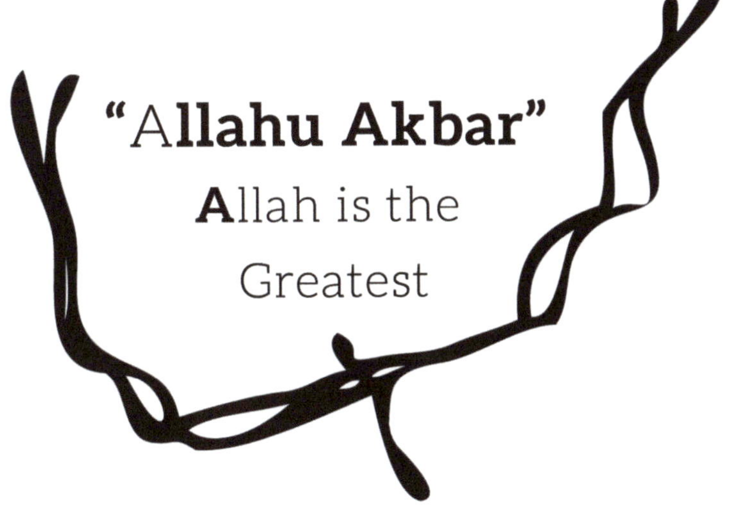
"Allahu Akbar"
Allah is the
Greatest

"La Ilaha illa
There is no God except
Allah"
Allah

And when you set forth in the land, then on you is not sin lest you shorten from the prayer, if you feared that of those who-who denied slay you. Truly, the deniers were a plain enemy to you... And when you were among them, then you established for them the prayer, so surely, a faction among them rise with you, and surely, they take their arms. Then when they prostrated themselves, so surely, they be behind you, and surely, another faction come of who pray not. So surely, they pray with you, and surely, they take their precaution... Then remember **A**llah in rising and seated and on your sides. Then when you reassured yourselves, then establish prayer. Truly, the prayer was upon the believers an appointed Decree...

Sura An-Nisa | The Women 4:101-103

Oh whichever be here of those who-who believed, when from the day of Friday it was called for prayer, then chase for the Remembrance of **A**llah and leave behind the sale. That is better for you, if you were knowing. Then when the prayer was concluded, then be dispersed in the land and seek from the Grace of **A**llah and remember **A**llah much, perhaps you prosper.

Sura Al Jumuah | The Friday 62:9-10

www.ingramcontent.com/pod-product-compliance
Ingram Content Group UK Ltd.
Pitfield, Milton Keynes, MK11 3LW, UK
UKHW060406300726
14090UKWH00006B/460

* 9 7 8 3 9 5 0 4 8 6 2 8 5 *